The Collection
2025

compiled by John Field

EXPRESS NEWSPAPERS

C CASSELL

First published in Great Britain in 2024 by Cassell,
an imprint of Octopus Publishing Group Ltd
Carmelite House
50 Victoria Embankment
London EC4Y 0DZ
www.octopusbooks.co.uk

An Hachette UK Company
www.hachette.co.uk

Cartoons supplied by British Cartoon Archive
Cartoons compiled by John Field

ISBN 978-1-78840-462-4

A CIP catalogue record for this book is available from the British Library.

Printed and bound in China.

1 3 5 7 9 10 8 6 4 2

Contents

Public Services

This year's collection of Carl Giles's cartoons covers six public services, all of which play a significant role in British life. They are Hospital Staff, Transport Workers, Law & Order, the Military, Politicians and Local Government.

Giles looked at news stories about these important and essential services through the eyes of a cartoonist and, consequently, frequently found a humorous angle on which to base a cartoon. However, he could also use a cartoon to make a serious comment when the news related to an issue which troubled him. It is clear, for example, that he disliked things such as football hooliganism, vandalism generally and racism, and sometimes he used his cartoons to express his strong feelings on these issues.

He could also be quite mischievous in his comments and drawings when portraying things such as the pomposity of a self-important person, or scenes in which a well-meaning public official or harassed police officer is overwhelmed by the situation they find themselves in.

The cartoons included in this collection have been chosen because they portray the wide range of situations facing public service figures as they go about their daily business. They also to illustrate Giles's great skill at finding a humorous side to almost any news item or storyline, and his innate ability to capture that humour on paper.

Hospital Staff

Over the years, Giles spent several periods in Ipswich Hospital and, no doubt, his experiences there allowed him to accurately capture various aspects of ward life in his hospital cartoons – some of which appear in this collection. These cartoons sometimes included characters based on actual doctors and nurses who he had met on the wards, and I understand that he became quite a popular patient with both. For many years, he provided an appropriate cartoon, based on a hospital theme, for the Nurses' magazine. Often his cartoons are centred upon the trials and tribulations of a patient, who is almost always male when it is a hospital scene.

Transport Workers

This chapter covers a range of workers in the transport sector, but Giles particularly loved drawing railway scenes, with all the comings and goings of people and locomotives. In his railway cartoons, he often focused on the difficulties that railway staff were confronted with, such as passengers' anger at railway strikes or problems of overcrowding on the railway system.

Law & Order

No doubt, Giles felt a great deal of respect for the exponents of law and order. However, at the same time, in his cartoons he could not resist creating such things as an outdoor crowd scene where the police have completely lost control of an unruly street demonstration, or where they are being outsmarted by a group of young children. Cartoons included in this chapter cover the police, judges, lawyers, prison staff and "villains" – out on the street or inside a courtroom or prison.

Military

Having spent the last eight months of World War II as a War Cartoonist – on the front line with the British Army as war swept across Europe from Belgium into Germany – Giles developed a great respect for all servicemen. He also gained detailed knowledge of army uniforms and equipment, and went to great lengths to ensure that his cartoons portrayed these as accurately as possible. Although Giles respected all ranks, he sometimes portrayed sympathy for the ordinary "Squaddie", irrespective of his "crime", when confronted with the powers of the officer class.

Politicians

Given how often they feature in his cartoon work, Giles seemed to have considered the seat of Parliament at Westminster, and those who inhabited it, as a regular source of inspiration. Although, privately, he may have held political beliefs, he rarely used a cartoon to express a strong political opinion. He did not shy away, however, from depicting politicians, including Prime Ministers, if the story required it.

This year's collection of Giles's cartoons focus in on six of Britain's key public services. They have been chosen to demonstrate his ability to frequently find an element of humour in an otherwise serious piece of news, or to make a pertinent comment on its storyline. Taken together, these cartoons provide a comprehensive record of life in the United Kingdom for almost half a century and depict public services that all still play a significant role in contemporary British life – I believe this is why Giles's drawings still have meaning for us today.

John Field

Local Government

Giles often produced political cartoons at the time of parliamentary or local elections. It is clear that he could not resist capturing the sense of high feelings which he felt existed between competing candidates at such times, whether nationwide or local. He enjoyed the idea of candidates from opposing parties squabbling like children in the period running up to an election, and even outside the voting booths on election day.

Hospital Staff

Any of the football fans who managed to convince the doctor they deserved a medical certificate and made it to Wembley to see England play Hungary that day would be stunned, like the rest of the nation, by Hungary's 6–3 victory.

"Let them in, nurse. One genuine flu – one genuine pimples – and the rest look like medical certificates for today's big match."

Daily Express, 25 November 1953

Earlier in the month, on 1 March 1954, the United States had tested a hydrogen bomb on Bikini Atoll in the Marshall Islands.

"I think I'll tell 'em they're all radio-active – just for fun."

Sunday Express, 28 March 1954

12 This depiction of the "joys" of Christmas in hospital has Giles's eye for adding plenty of amusing detail, including a lusty and unappreciated rendition of "Silent Night".

Dedicated to all those compelled to spend Christmas in hospital, where there is little or no escape from giving a hand with the decorations. I know, I've had some.

Daily Express, 24 December 1954

On 10 July 1957, the Guernsey Board of Health fired 12 nurses who had gone on hunger strike the previous day. When the Transport and General Workers' Union threatened action, a court of inquiry recommended that all be reinstated.

An appeal has been made for every nurse to be off duty during the inquiry into the Nurses v. Hospital Authorities dispute in Guernsey.

Daily Express, 16 July 1957

14   This was during a period of heightened tensions during the Cold War. Reassurance from the United States not to fear Nikita Khrushchev, leader of the Soviet Union, was not enough for these many patients, including Vera and George Junior.

"Nothing brings 'em out in spots quicker than an assurance from the States like: 'Don't be frightened of Khrushchev. We will come to your aid.'"

Daily Express, 12 May 1960

The findings of an inquiry into the problem of noise control in hospitals published in November 1958, with a follow-up in 1960, said that sound, including squeaking wheels and chattering nurses, could impact patients' recovery. Following this, the Ministry of Health produced anti-noise posters to be displayed in hospitals.

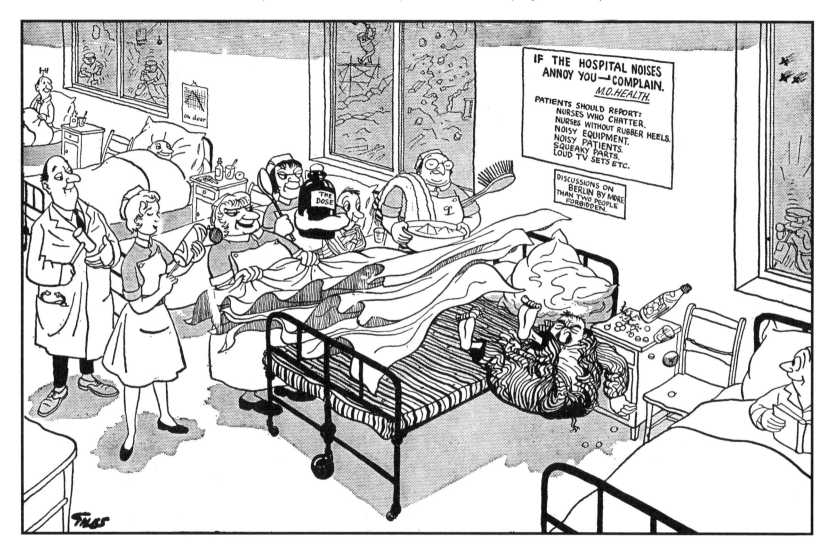

"You the one who complained to Matron about us making a noise?"

Sunday Express, 20 August 1961

16   A London research centre had begun experiments in keeping patients suspended in mid-air with the aim of advancing the treatment of burn victims.

"In this ward we're trying this 'Floating patients on air' experiment you've been reading about."

Sunday Express, 26 November 1961

In 1962, nurses launched a major protest over pay levels and were eventually given a special pay award. Matron – still very much a figure to fear and respect in the early 1960s – isn't best pleased about this nurse's chosen way to celebrate that.

"Someone told Matron you celebrated your pay increase and came back and gave 'em all a double dose of pep pills."

Sunday Express, 9 September 1962

18	It may be the first day of spring but many still seem to be suffering ill health after the Big Freeze of winter 1962–63, one of the coldest on record.

"Hey ho, first day of spring – all those who haven't got Asian flu have got gastro-enteritis."

Daily Express, 21 March 1963

Clearly the nurses' charms are very effective when it comes receiving enthusiastic assistance in decking the halls – and wards.

"If you're fit enough to do the decorating around here you're fit enough to come home and do ours."

Daily Express, 17 December 1963

From 1970, the *Daily Express* sponsored the Nurse of the Year Contest, in which candidates were nominated and voted for by readers.

"Talk about vote chasing – you only have to 'oller 'Nurse!' nowadays and they come for you like a swarm of bees."

Daily Express, 12 March 1970

"Mixed wards aren't curing me very quick, with these two ding-donging next to me all day."

Daily Express, 2 February 1971

22 In October 1972, the Briggs Report – a review of nursing and the changing healthcare system – recommended, among other things, that the age of entry to nursing training be lowered.

"This is your new nurse – Henrietta. She lied about her age to serve her country, she's only twelve."

Daily Express, 19 October 1972

The Cod Wars were a series of conflicts between Britain and Iceland regarding fishing rights in the North Atlantic between the late 1950s and 1976. The previous day, the media had reported that the Government had met with cod trawlermen.

"I know I should be grateful in my nice warm bed, but I bet the poor harassed cod men don't have the damn stuff steamed day in day out."

Sunday Express, 21 January 1973

It's not clear what Nurse Rigg intends to do with the brush, but she is clearly looking forward to patching up these football supporters. The previous day, Giles's team, Ipswich Town, had lost 3–2 away to Leeds United.

"Nurse Rigg here will patch you up, she's very good with football riff-raff. Her team lost yesterday, by the way."

Sunday Express, 21 April 1974

In the early 1970s, "pay beds" in NHS hospitals, made available for consultants to treat their private patients, caused resentment among workers and were increasingly targeted by unions. In addition, reforms by the Government concerning consultants' right to hold private clinics alongside their NHS work led to a dispute.

"Awake, luv? The consultant said he'll be back to stitch you up in about a fortnight."

Daily Express, 6 July 1974

This unfortunate patient's Christmas has just gone from bad to worse.

"Now who do you think has come all the way across the country to cheer you up?"

Sunday Express, 15 December 1974

It is to be hoped that the formidable-looking doctor has not overheard the nurse's joke at her expense.

"Here comes Doctor – clad in a see-through bikini in peacock blue and flamingo pink."

Daily Express, 30 August 1975

28   In 1975, doctors officially went on strike for the first time in the history of the NHS. Junior doctors and consultants withdrew all but emergency services.

"He says his case is urgent. He's been feeling a bit depressed since September 29 1905."

Daily Express, 20 October 1975

January 1979, in what came to be known as the "Winter of Discontent", was brutally chilly, with much of the UK experiencing long cold spells with heavy snowfall.

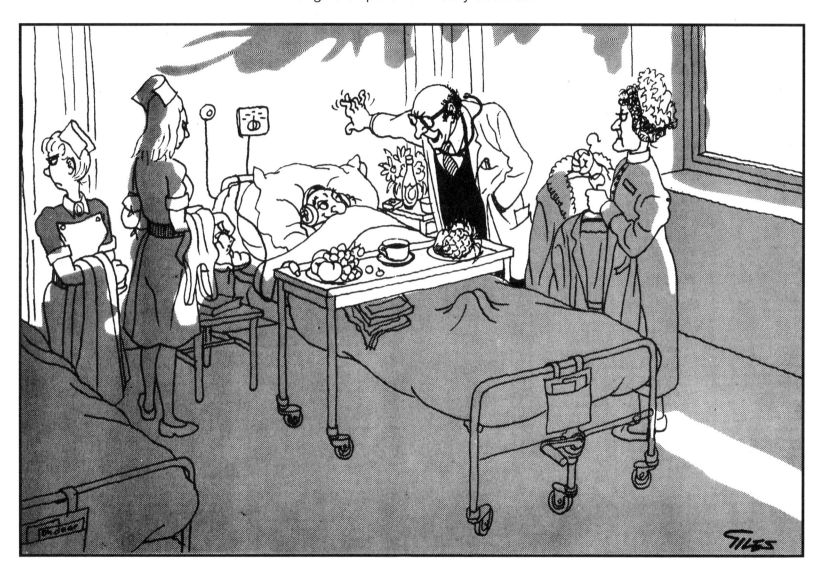

"Sister tells me those mysterious pains you came to us about on the first fall of snow have just as mysteriously disappeared with the thaw."

Daily Express, 9 January 1979

In 1979, a referendum on a devolved assembly for Scotland fell short of the 40 per cent "yes" vote required. A second referendum held in 1997 led to the creation of a devolved Scottish parliament in 1999.

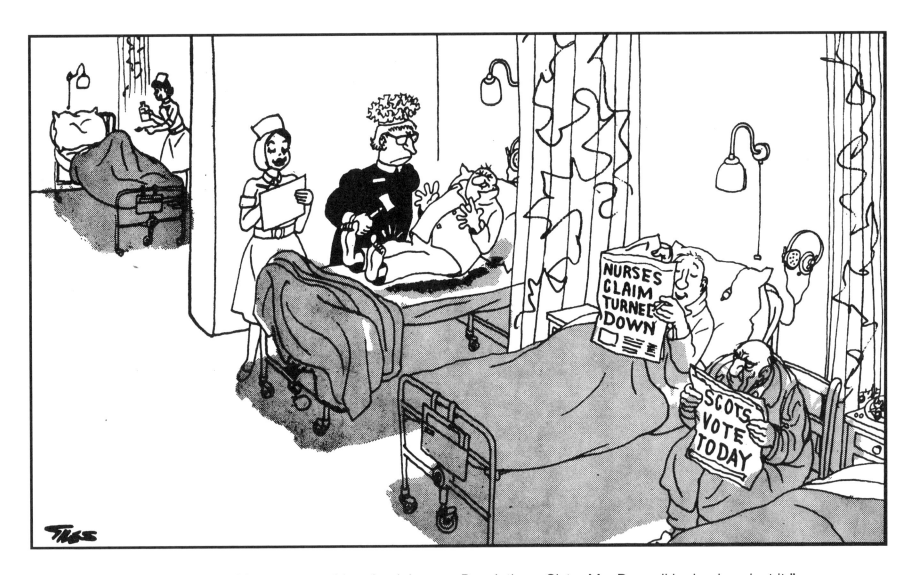

"I'd refrain from airing your considered opinions on Devolution – Sister MacDougall is dead against it."

Daily Express, 1 March 1979

Tradition says that Christmas decorations should come down on Twelfth Night to avoid bad luck. But it appears the patients are out of luck anyway…

"Everybody up! Decorations down! And I warn you we're not very happy with our wage settlement."

Sunday Express, 6 January 1980

Between 1977 and 1983, carrier pigeons were used to transport laboratory specimen vials between two hospitals in Devon.

"Nurse, you will inform your ward that the new pigeon service is not installed for the passing of betting slips."

Sunday Express, 20 January 1980

Having argued unsuccessfully for a 12 per cent salary increase, these nurses understandably take a dim view of other, more generous, public sector pay awards.

"Oh boy! These two are mine – one civil servant at 14.3%, and one judge at 18.6% wage increase!"

Sunday Express, 16 May 1982

34   The US Presidential Election had taken place on 4 November, while in the UK the by-election for the seat vacated by Robert Kilroy Silk, then a Labour MP, was due two days later, and political parties were already gearing up for the 1987 General Election.

"We're sorry about the extra hour's wait – Doctor's had an epidemic of election fever."

Daily Express, 11 November 1986

If poetry and flowers – which look suspiciously like they may have been sourced from the vase at the patient's bedside – won't work, perhaps the champagne will.

"It's a beautiful poem of undying love, the flowers are wonderful, but I'm still not letting you have a fiver till Friday."

Sunday Express, 26 April 1987

36   The din in this baby clinic is going to become even worse as an unknown hand, seen in the bottom left, is about to pull away the trolley.

"Just try me with a free ticket to send him to Australia until he's forty"

Sunday Express, 23 October 1988

These nurses evidently have little sympathy with a recent headline that declared, "Junior doctors overworked say junior doctors",   37
and are only too pleased to wake the hapless medic to assist in removing the children's costumes.

"Wakey, wakey – the lady's little boys can't get their Garfield and Odie suits off."

Daily Express, 3 January 1989

38 As with many of Giles's cartoons about nurses, this one illustrates that they were perennially underpaid and overworked – look at the stream of patients in the background.

"Over here, Fireworks – they're paying me an extra sixpence to keep you in fitness and in health."

Sunday Express, 19 February 1989

Transport Workers

In 1947, the newly nationalized railway system badly needed to improve rolling stock damaged and neglected in the war, but these are desperate measures.

"Good afternoon. We're from the Ministry of Rail Transport. I suppose you've heard that the country needs all the rolling-stock that is available?"

Sunday Express, 7 December 1947

In 1952, increases in bus fares were implemented in London from 2 March and in the rest of the country from 1 May.

"Bloomin' shame – can't afford two bus fares now, so the poor little wife has to walk."

Sunday Express, 2 March 1952

In January 1954, the newspapers were full of the story of the elopement of 20-year-old Sir James Goldsmith and 17-year-old Bolivian heiress María Isabel Patiño, daughter of one of the world's richest men.

"On your feet, Cupid – we've got a flat tyre."

Daily Express, 8 January 1954

42

The prospect of their moment in the spotlight has spurred these railway workers into a special effort to spruce up themselves – and the sandwiches.

"Well, ever since they heard the B.B.C. were talking of televising the black spots of British Railways..."

Daily Express, 15 February 1955

The 1955 FA Cup Final was played on 7 May between Newcastle United and Manchester City, the same day as motor racing's International Trophy at Silverstone, as these unlucky City fans have discovered.

"Hang on a minute – I'll ask the gentleman behind if he'll back."

Daily Express, 7 May 1955

44   The sergeant appears as unimpressed as the bus driver and conductor at the way the Highway Code has been enforced for this "illegally parked" bus.

"Parked on a bus stop so we roped him in."

Daily Express, 3 May 1957

This irate trainless passenger is making clear her thoughts on the ill-timed attempt to drum up support for the National Union of Railwaymen dance.

"I must say Harry's picked a poor time to sell her a ticket for the N.U.R. dance."

Daily Express, 11 February 1960

46 By the 1960s, steam trains were largely gone from the rails, replaced by more efficient diesel locomotives, so the steam-engine driver might relish this chance to mock mechanical failure.

"If he comes his 'Ho, ho, ho, what's up, battery flat?' I'm going to dot him."

Sunday Express, 15 January 1961

Until the Great Train Robbery two years after this cartoon, Britain had experienced only minor robberies on the rail network and Harry is making very sure the mailbags in his care are safe. Stinker, as he can often be seen doing in Giles's cartoons, is recording the episode.

"We've got to get it into Harry's head that everybody in a wheelchair isn't after his mailbags."

Daily Express, 30 March 1961

The Beeching Cuts, named after Dr Richard Beeching, then chairman of the British Railways Board, were the result of two infamous reports that identified thousands of stations and lines for closure in the 1960s.

"Bert's got a point there – if you're so keen on the express stopping here why can't you use your missus instead of his?"

Sunday Express, 24 June 1962

Two days before this cartoon and seven months before the publication of his first report, Dr Beeching (see page 48) was greeted by a crowd of protesting railway maintenance workers at Edinburgh Waverley station, one of who aimed a kick at him.

"Never mind about Dr. Beeching not complaining about being kicked – I am!"

Daily Express, 30 August 1962

The first of Dr Beeching's reports, entitled The Reshaping of British Railways, was published the day before this cartoon (see page 48).

"Dr. Beeching's plan to streamline the railways don't provide separate freight for Lady Ringboan's 'orse."

Daily Express, 28 March 1963

"Witty remarks about where you think the Beeching axe ought to fall first won't get you over any quicker, I might tell you."

Daily Express, 18 February 1965

Perhaps this milkman should have been less keen to advertise the advantages of a milk float over other goods vehicles.

"Goodness! So we have."

Daily Express, 24 June 1965

"I always go up to the Motor Show by train because the roads are too crowded."

Daily Express, 21 October 1965

The previous day, newspapers had said that the London Transport Board was considering recruiting female bus drivers.

"That's only one hazard – her Ronnie ain't well enough to go to school so he has to come to work with her."

Daily Express, 22 February 1966

Feisty Grandma, with only the ever-poorly Vera to help carry their luggage, challenges any of the porters who may be considering turning blackleg to assist the beauty.

"I dare any one of you."

Daily Express, 29 June 1967

Yet another strike to feature in headlines and in a Giles cartoon – the previous day, rail signalmen had threatened industrial action.

"The fact that Brother's holiday falls at the same time as our unofficial strike is Brother's bleedin' hard luck."

Daily Express, 30 May 1969

The previous day, Tottenham Hotspur supporters, having damaged the train carrying them back from a defeat at Derby, had been ejected from it at Flitwick in Bedfordshire where they created a major disturbance. This Giles cartoon suggests this alternative "no-frills" form of rail transport for football fans.

"The management apologises for the absence of glass, seat, communication cords, etc. but hopes that you will occupy your tiny minds with holding on."

Daily Express, 23 September 1969

58 The day before, newspapers had reported that a London–New York service on low-budget airline Laker Airways, with fares as low as £32.50 one way, had been approved by the Civil Aviation Authority.

"Gentleman says he got hold of three nice pieces of skate. He'd like two well done and young Archie would like his medium."

Daily Express, 28 September 1972

British Rail began running trials of its prototype for a new high-speed diesel train, the InterCity 125, in autumn 1972.

"We don't have problems with 150 m.p.h. supertrains on our line, do we Harry?"

Daily Express, 21 November 1972

60 Football specials – trains specifically for supporters with reasonably priced tickets – were beginning to be phased out at this point in the 1970s. Luckily, this ticket-office clerk has his fierce guard dog to protect him from angry away fans.

"Protection, mate. First sign of aggro out of any of 'em and pow!!"

Daily Express, 17 August 1974

Sid has rolled out the red carpet on the off-chance that Princess Anne, the Princess Royal – who in 1974 became the first member of the Royal Family to have an HGV licence – might be passing by and in need of refreshment.

"Didn't you read? Princess Anne's passed her heavy goods vehicle driving test."

Daily Express, 15 October 1974

62   In the 1970s, despite British Rail singing the praises of the "The Age of the Train", many commuters faced morning misery with uncomfortable old rolling stock and lack of space.

"As senior executive of the accounts department, under no circumstances whatsoever will I sit on your lap."

Daily Express, 11 September 1975

In 1976, commuters were increasingly frustrated by fare increases which were the result of the Government placing a cap on subsidizing unprofitable British Rail. It is questionable though whether Harry's bird impressions will help…

"It's up to us to make the commuters think the new increase is all worth while. How about a cheerful Monday-morning smile and a few of your bird noises, Harry?"

Sunday Express, 31 October 1976

One suspects the chef's third guess – that it is neither a food-standards inspector nor food critic Egon Ronay, but a haulier with pretensions – is correct.

"It's either a Ministry of Transport spy, Egon Ronay, or one of 'em coming it."

Daily Express, 28 November 1977

British Rail's new fast freight service, Speedlink, was launched in September 1977 as an attempt to improve its freight business.

"I told the old fool it wouldn't stop for a birthday card to her sister in New York!"

Daily Express, 2 June 1978

To ensure better timekeeping, British Rail had issued staff with free watches.

"They gave Fred an alarm clock to wake him up to let him know he's arrived."

Sunday Express, 8 January 1984

"Looks as if we're going to be here for a long time – how about joining in singing The Merry Month of May?

Sunday Express, 1 May 1988

Law & Order

"Lost property", Ernie, Stinker, George Junior and the twins are creating their customary mayhem.

"Sergeant, we want reinforcements or extra pay for looking after this lot until someone claims 'em."

Daily Express, 13 August 1955

Banned in the UK, the novel *Lady Chatterley's Lover* was the subject of an obscenity trial in 1960, the jury famously acquitting publisher Penguin, thus overturning the ban.

"Just listen to all those 'Cors!' and 'Oos!' and long low whistles."

Sunday Express, 23 October 1960

The recommendations of a Royal Commission in 1960 led to significant pay increases for police officers.

"Since they've heard about our pay increase this is the third time I've been slugged and had me wallet whipped."

Sunday Express, 27 November 1960

These police officers are hoping to demonstrate just how over-zealous they can be. 71

"Just leave it there one minute over time my lad – that's all."

Daily Express, 7 February 1961

72   In March 1963, Christine Keeler – whose affair with Secretary of State John Profumo created a scandal that helped topple the Conservative Government – failed to appear as a witness in an Old Bailey trial and was found living in Madrid.

"While the witness is giving evidence for the prosecution I must ask the defendant not to keep interrupting with 'Why don't you clear off to Madrid?'"

Daily Express, 26 March 1963

On 22 December 1965, a temporary speed limit of 70 mph was introduced on British roads. The limit was extended in 1966 and made permanent in 1967.

"You're in luck, lads – the Bench are all Rally drivers who don't approve of the 70 m.p.h. maximum."

Daily Express, 30 December 1965

74   It had recently been reported that, under plans to amalgamate police forces to reduce their number, Chief Constables who had been replaced might be given a new rank.

"Bit early to be using language like 'Here's your tea, Fred.' The Chief hasn't been axed yet."

On 17 March 1968, an anti-Vietnam War protest outside the US Embassy in London's Grosvenor Square had turned violent, with some 25 police officers taken to hospital. A newspaper report on 20 April had revealed that police had been called to a Glasgow school following a riot by pupils over school dinners.

"All yours – two dozen school meal rioters and you can give me a Grosvenor Square any time."

Sunday Express, 21 April 1968

76   Passing the death sentence on this repeat offender appears to be a satisfactory outcome to the traffic warden. Fortunately for the driver, the death sentence for all but treason had been abolished the previous year in the UK.

"For allowing your car to be left 3 minutes beyond the allotted time on a yellow line twice in one year there is no punishment too severe. It is therefore my duty..."

Daily Express, 19 March 1970

British lawyer, influential political advisor and Chairman of the Arts Council of Great Britain at the time, Lord Arnold Goodman, had said that the legal profession had "an absolutely demented professional structure".

"I am aware of Lord Goodman's opinion that the British Legal System is 'Demented,' nevertheless this boy did wilfully commit the serious crime of acquiring sixpennyworth of sweets after legal shopping hours."

Sunday Express, 27 September 1970

A police campaign had been launched against rings of car thieves shipping stolen vehicles to the Continent. The church in the background is St Mary-le-Tower in Giles's hometown Ipswich, with St Lawrence in the distance.

"Don't congratulate <u>me</u> on taking all reasonable precautions to immobilise my car – they've nicked my wheels."

Daily Express, 30 September 1971

"He says if Tommy Docherty is speaking up for us what are the Fuzz beefing about?"

Daily Express, 20 August 1974

80   Sir Robert Mark, Commissioner of the Metropolitan Police, had complained that he thought the courts were too lenient. His Dimbleby Lecture two years earlier, in which he was fiercely critical of corrupt members of the legal profession, had caused a nationwide scandal and provoked indignation among lawyers.

"Should cheer the cockles of your little hearts, lads – Sir Robert Mark's attack on magistrates for being too lenient has sent them all 'opping mad."

Sunday Express, 9 November 1975

Giles depicts judges settling their difference in a bout of fisticuffs, rather than the more sedate verbal spat reported in the papers between Sir John Widgery, Lord Chief Justice of England and Wales, and a member of the judiciary.

"'Ullo, 'ullo, 'ullo!"

Sunday Express, 22 February 1976

A football fan, Giles abhorred the hooliganism and violence that marred the sport in the 1970s.

"You say it all stems from your unhappy childhood. Your mummy wouldn't let you have a teddy bear, so at precisely one minute after kick-off you decided to boot a policeman in the face."

Daily Express, 31 August 1976

Having read the depressing headlines, this prisoner clearly thinks he is better off remaining a guest of Her Majesty's Prison Service.

83

"Now don't you come in here bailing me out."

Sunday Express, 10 October 1976

84 Even the most optimistic punter would be unlikely to bet on largesse from the judge in this instance.

"Yes, I did read of the judge who paid £8.95 damages to avoid a lengthy and expensive trial, but I wouldn't count on him paying the £1,500 you 'borrowed' from your firm to put on a horse."

Daily Express, 4 February 1977

Newspapers had reported a judge stating that, in his opinion, sex under the age of 16 was immoral but not criminal.

"They all read much the same – Dear Judge, as you don't think it's illegal, you can have 'em."

Daily Express, 14 February 1977

A judge had recently been reported as saying he would have the ears off offenders if he could.

"Oh dear, you've got a right one this morning – he won't only have your ears off!"

Daily Express, 6 February 1978

Grandma has a dim of view of the neighbour's poodle and the judge has an equally dim view of the merits of this case.

"The Prosecution claims this lady did throw a cabbage at her neighbour's poodle who was trespassing upon her lawn.
How the devil did this get to the High Court?"

Daily Express, 7 December 1978

Messrs Blok and Blok are an unlikely duo to be compared to popular athletes and archrivals Sebastian Coe and Steve Ovett.

"Action stations! Sebastian Coe and Steve Ovett back from lunch."

Daily Express, 4 October 1979

From 2 January 1980, British Steel Corporation workers throughout the country went on strike to support a demand for a 20 per cent pay rise. In February there were ugly picket line scenes and several arrests at a large production plant in Yorkshire after employees there voted to return to work.

"I don't suppose it will affect his judgement although it was his parked car you kicked in and one of you broke his son-in-law's nose."

Daily Express, 21 February 1980

90   During the prison warders' dispute in 1980, many prisons refused to accept prisoners newly sentenced by the courts, leading to thousands of prisoners being held in police cells.

"'We can't make a cup of tea like they do in the Scrubs'."

Daily Express, 23 October 1980

Recently, members of a rugby club at a carnival had de-skirted WPC Anne Pitman, who was on duty at the carnival, after hoisting her onto the float they were on.

"Well I'm damned – so they have!"

Sunday Express, 2 November 1980

92   The Scarman Report, commissioned by the Government following the riots in Brixton in April 1981 and published the day before this cartoon, had emphasized the need for police consultation with local communities.

"Don't go away son – me and my mate are just going to have consultation whether we thump your head or kick your backside."

Daily Express, 26 November 1981

A jury at the Old Bailey had recently been given 24-hour police protection.

93

"There are enough sitting down for meals in this house without your four jury bodyguards."

Daily Express, 14 September 1982

Crime levels rose sharply in Britain in the early 1980s at a time when unemployment was also soaring. Unemployment as a mitigating factor is unlikely to make the judge any more sympathetic in this instance though.

"I wouldn't bank on M'Lud letting you off because you are unemployed – it happened to be his pad which you did up."

Sunday Express, 18 March 1984

It doesn't appear that the defendant has much ground for optimism in this case.

"If you exercise your right to dismiss the jury – the plaintiff confesses it was he who attacked you, and the Judge is in a good mood – we might just have a chance."

Daily Express, 3 December 1985

The 1980s was a decade of stringent government cuts to funding and above-inflation fare rises on British Rail. Add repeated industrial disputes to that and it is little wonder that everyone was disenchanted with the service.

"You won't get off light with this one – he sentenced one of 'em yesterday to six months travel on B.R."

Daily Express, 5 February 1987

Giles is poking fun, in his inimitable fashion, following a recent newspaper heading stating, "Court orders boy to walk to school".

"Her council won't give her boy a car to go fishing during the holidays – how the hell did this get as far as the Appeal Court?"

Daily Express, 16 April 1987

Judge Pickles, renowned for his controversial sentencing, had just made headlines for jailing a young woman who was too afraid of her boyfriend to give evidence against him in an assault case.

"Failing to tell Judge Pickles why you refuse to wear your new shoes could land you in prison for a very long time."

Daily Express, 14 March 1989

Military

The Giles family – among them Grandma in the unlikely role of pilot – are enjoying the 1952 Farnborough Airshow, which was marred by a tragic air accident a few days after this cartoon was published. The British aviation industry was beginning to thrive following the war.

"If we sell all our best planes to America and they send 'em back to bases in England, I reckon that's good business."

Daily Express, 4 September 1952

Research during World War II had led to the creation of the first supersonic jets and these demonstrations of their abilities and their characteristic sonic boom are not popular with the landlord.

"Supersonic bang demonstrations are costing me something in glasses."

Daily Express, 3 September 1953

How very unfortunate for the soldiers that their companion's voice has carried over the sound of the jazz band in this nightclub.

"*I* don't think your sergeant's a pig, I think he's cute."

Daily Express, 25 August 1954

102 A debate in Parliament three days earlier had discussed the difficulty of finding enough stowage for beer onboard Navy ships. It had been calculated, by way of example, that enough beer to provide one pint per sailor for 28 days on the aircraft carrier HMS *Indomitable* would weigh 43.6 tons (39.5 tonnes).

"Cap'n – you wanna tell that bloke in Parliament who said the Navy's gonna get more beer if they can find the space that we're full right up."

Sunday Express, 6 March 1955

"He's hiding in my tree."

Daily Express, 26 October 1956

104   Following this ill-advised remark, most of the drinkers feel discretion is definitely the better part of valour when faced by irate Marines and move sharply towards the exit en masse.

"Who ever heard of a Marine who could march, anyway?"

Daily Express, 3 November 1959

Freezing conditions means the end of National Service – which was to come on 31 December 1960 – is all too far away for this camp guard.

105

"If you see the Colonel tell him you've got a volunteer willing to reduce our armed forces by 1."

Sunday Express, 17 January 1960

On 31 August, the German Democratic Republic, or East Germany, had begun constructing the Berlin Wall, which stood until 1989.

"Excuse me – I think you've still got one of my chaps over there."

Daily Express, 21 November 1961

A curfew had been imposed on unmarried British soldiers following violent incidents between British soldiers and civilians stationed in Minden and Schneverdingen in what was then West Germany.

"Now to find the Cinderella whose tiny foot fits this little boot."

Daily Express, 28 June 1962

In July 1963, the government proposed the establishment of a unified Ministry of Defence with complete authority for the Armed Forces invested in a single Secretary of State. One of the aims of the merger – perhaps optimistically, judging by this cartoon – was to curb interservice rivalries.

"The Navy said he wasn't going to wear a bearskin and the R.A.F. said he was damned if he was going to wear spurs. That started it."

Daily Express, 18 July 1963

Armed conflict between Greek and Turkish Cypriots broke out in December 1963 and a force of 2,700 British soldiers was deployed to help enforce a ceasefire. Small wonder that these troops are far happier to find themselves in foggy Manchester.

"Men, I know you will all be disappointed to learn that because of the fog we have been diverted from Cyprus to Manchester."

Sunday Express, 29 December 1963

110   When China intervened in the Korean War in late 1950, the United States issued a total trade embargo that wasn't lifted until 1972, an embargo that these American military police are determined to enforce.

"I'm afraid he asked for it – helping China's war effort by exporting six dozen Mickey Mice to Shanghai."

Daily Express, 12 May 1964

Rumours of possible cuts to the British Army of the Rhine (BAOR) stationed in West Germany that had circulated in recent newspapers had just been denied.

"Sergeant's going to be cross with Harry. The rumour that we're being withdrawn from Germany has been denied."

Daily Express, 1 December 1964

112　From the early 1960s, a shortage of medical personnel in the Navy meant that women doctors were able to work on short-term contracts, although women weren't allowed to go to sea until some 30 years later.

"Never did so many diseases suddenly break out among so many."

Daily Express, 30 November 1965

London Zoo's favourite attraction, Chi-Chi the giant panda, was sent to Moscow in 1966 in the hopes of mating her with An-An, another captive giant panda. Romance didn't blossom, however.

"I'll laugh if comrade An-An has flipped off to Peking when this Chi-Chi gets to Moscow."

Daily Express, 10 March 1966

114   US President Richard Nixon made a brief visit to London in February 1969, attending a luncheon at Buckingham Palace given in his honour. BBC2 had launched colour television in 1967.

"Now I've seen everything. Powdering their little red noses for colour TV."

Sunday Express, 23 February 1969

"Right ho, chaps – the Royal Romance is officially denied. You will now cut cards for the privilege of ordering a whip-round for the wedding present."

Daily Express, 25 September 1973

116 In October 1973, Arab members of the Organization of Petroleum Exporting Countries (OPEC) imposed an embargo on countries, including the United Kingdom, that had supported Israel in the Fourth Arab–Israeli War. The embargo banned petroleum exports to those countries and cut oil production, resulting in petrol rationing.

"The age old custom of flogging Army equipment is one thing, the disposal of the Queen's coach horses to would-be petrol economists is another."

Daily Express, 30 October 1973

The wedding of Princess Anne and Mark Phillips was declared a special bank holiday. Their elaborately decorated five-tier wedding cake reportedly weighed a hefty 145 pounds (65.7kg). (See the cartoon on page 115.)

"I trust the ingredients of our bangers and beans have been mixed with the same loving care as HRH's cake."

Sunday Express, 11 November 1973

"Male chauvinist pig" was a disparaging description coined by feminists in the late 1960s.

"Here comes a male chauvinist pig if ever I saw one."

Daily Express, 15 June 1974

Earlier in the month, a group of ships had called into South Africa – the Royal Navy had a long-standing agreement for the use of a naval base at Simon's Town near Cape Town.

"It's not so much what the British government might think about the Navy's visit to South Africa – it's what some of their missuses might think."

Sunday Express, 27 October 1974

120 For a period in 1975 Prince Charles, now King Charles, sported a moustache in contravention of Navy regulations permitting only a "full set" of moustache and beard, not one without the other.

"His Royal Highness busting Queen's Regulations is one thing – Ordinary Seaman Jones busting 'em is another. GIT IT ORF!"

Daily Express, 30 May 1975

During the Cod Wars, the long-lasting conflict between Iceland and Britain concerning rights to fish in Icelandic waters, the Royal Navy sent warships to the North Atlantic to protect British fishing trawlers.

"And sweetheart – stop calling me your 'little Jaws' in front of the lads."

Daily Express, 25 November 1975

Prince Charles's naval career ended in December 1976, with the rank of Commander. No doubt, these sailors wish they could follow suit.

"Why anyone should want to quit the Navy beats me."

Daily Express, 21 September 1976

A United States Army General had referred to the British Army as "all bands and ceremonials".

"In view of the American general's observations on the British Forces we will omit the first two bars of 'Colonel Bogey'."

Daily Express, 21 October 1976

The Household Guards are wisely resorting to slippers and whispers to avoid waking five-day-old Peter Phillips, Princess Anne's first child.

"By the left, quick march – pass it on."

Sunday Express, 20 November 1977

"You should get a splendid view of Trooping The Colour from there, madam – you're on the exact spot where Her Majesty will be taking the salute."

Daily Express, 12 June 1980

126 It's unlikely "Auntie Serg." will be offering the sympathetic ear and helpful advice usually associated with newspaper agony aunts.

"Wait till you see your 'agony aunt' before you start writing."

Daily Express, 28 January 1988

Politicians

Labour was returned to power, with a much slimmer majority, in the General Election on 23 February.

"Well, Madam, if you have definitely decided not to vote for me what am I doing nursing your baby?"

Sunday Express, 12 February 1950

128   A wry comment on the hypocrisy of campaigning politicians. The 1955 General Election took place a month after this cartoon.

"I like the way they tell you how they're going to grind their opponents in the dust in the same breath that they ask you to elect them as 'a man of peace'."

Daily Express, 26 April 1955

Weariness with politicians – and the weather – in the run-up to the 1955 General Election is evident. May had been particularly cold and wet and, two days before this cartoon, England and Wales experienced widespread snow and blizzard conditions.

"If we went where they told us, at least we shouldn't be getting snow in May."

Daily Express, 19 May 1955

Seated among the plotters in this pub, leek in his lapel, is Welsh Labour politician Aneurin "Nye" Bevan who had served as Health Minister in the previous Labour government.

"Listen, Dai. When we've got them nicely tied up on Suez, Cyprus, wages, cost of living, you stand up and start hollering Home Rule for Wales."

Sunday Express, 7 October 1956

Giles turns his creative drawing skills to imagining the scene that had inspired the previous day's headline.

131

No joke, no political motive. Simply an illustration to yesterday's fascinating headline: M.P.s IN PARIS BEG FOR MEAL.

Daily Express, 28 February 1957

132 This Conservative MP clearly feels insult is being added to injury by idle chat of football after what he perceives as filibustering – deliberately wasting time during a debate with an overlong speech or quibbling about procedural points to delay a motion or Bill.

"If there's a thing I dislike more than a Labour M.P. who filibusts me all night it's a Labour M.P. who thinks he's going to keep me another hour discussing his home team's chances in the Cup."

Sunday Express, 19 February 1961

These street traders are doing a roaring trade with MPs afraid of dozing off and making newspaper headlines.

Daily Express, 8 February 1962

The Liberal Party had won the Orpington by-election four days earlier, turning a government majority of 14,760 in the 1959 General Election into a Liberal one of 7,855.

"Forgetting for a moment those of you who voted Liberal, there is one among us who went the whole hog – voted Labour."

Sunday Express, 18 March 1962

"Rodney took some pretty silly bets in the bar last night about the strength of our future policies."

Daily Express, 11 October 1962

136   A recent demand for a pay increase by Conservative backbenchers had been unsuccessful but, as the police officer has kindly pointed out, protesting outside 10 Downing Street was pointless – it underwent major rebuilding work in the early 1960s, Prime Minister Harold Macmillan residing in Admiralty House until September 1963.

"You've chained yourself to the wrong railings, sir – the Prime Minister hasn't lived here since August 1960."

Daily Express, 11 April 1963

At the time that this cartoon was published, the results of the Vassall Tribunal were expected. The government inquiry aimed to discover if any ministers or civil servants were implicated following the unmasking of Admiralty civil servant John Vassall as a Soviet spy.

"Potential Guy Fawkes, the lot of you."

Daily Express, 16 April 1963

138 Canvassing in the run-up to the General Election, Sir Alec Douglas-Home – who served as Prime Minister for only 363 days – has run foul of this voter's enthusiastic dog.

"Madam! Your confounded dog has picked our Prime Minister up by his ears."

Daily Express, 30 April 1964

"If anything happens to me pray tell Sir Alec of the great lengths I went to to win youth over to our side."

Sunday Express, 6 September 1964

140 The previous day, Labour MPs, led by new Prime Minister Harold Wilson, had agreed to a delay in a promised increase in old-age pensions proposed by the National Insurance Bill.

"For goodness' sake get Wilson to give him his pension and let's have breakfast without him banging on the window with his 'You got yourn, wot about mine'."

Daily Express, 26 November 1964

A few days earlier, Harold Wilson's Labour government, in what was dubbed the "Sterling Crisis", had devalued the pound by 14 per cent, prompting "constructive heckling" by these Opposition backbenchers.

"I think your 'Yah boo' was frightfully good constructive criticism – What did you think of my 'Resign you cads, Yaroop!'?"

Daily Express, 23 November 1967

142 The Labour Party Conference was held in Brighton from 28 September to 3 October, shortly before the Conservative Conference. Conservative Quintin McGarel Hogg is not going to be tempted by the same room – and possibly an apple-pie bed – that had been allocated to Minister of Technology, Anthony "Tony" Wedgwood Benn.

"I'm damned if I'll pay double the money for the same lucky room that Wedgwood Benn had last week."

Daily Express, 7 October 1969

West German magazine *Stern* had alleged that a "high-ranking" British diplomat had become involved in a prostitution scandal. The diplomat, later confirmed to be an Under Secretary of State, was said to come from a well-known aristocratic family and to have access to many military secrets.

"If YOUR conscience is absolutely clear why are you pouring your coffee in your egg?"

Daily Express, 24 May 1973

Kissing babies is one of the perils of election campaigning. Jeremy Thorpe was leader of the Liberal Party at the time.

"Careful with this one – he had Jeremy Thorpe yesterday."

Daily Express, 12 February 1974

Earlier in the year one of the most serious corruption cases seen in Britain had ended in the imprisonment of architect, John Poulson, and civil servant, George Pottinger, and the conviction of other politicians, with investigations still ongoing at the time of this cartoon.

"Buying my secretary chocolate every day may well be considered as a bribe in high places."

Daily Express, 2 May 1974

Grandma, seen here with the family's dog Butch, is open to bit of bribery to encourage her to put her cross in the right box come the election.

"The last one put his coat down and bought me two gins and tonics."

Sunday Express, 6 October 1974

This man makes his opinion on having his privacy invaded by canvassers very clear.

"When I asked you where you would be putting your cross I was asking a perfectly civil question."

Sunday Express, 15 April 1979

Welsh Liberal politician David Lloyd George was Prime Minister from 1916 to 1922, the last time a Liberal held the post – an achievement unlikely to be repeated by these politicians, according to this chatty child's parent.

"My father says none of you've got a cat's chance in hell of being a Lloyd George."

Daily Express, 15 September 1981

Black Rod's most well-known duty is summoning MPs from the Commons to hear the King or Queen's Speech. The door is closed on Black Rod's approach and he or she must knock three times on the door with the rod before being admitted.

"It's not Black Rod, M'Lord – the lady has left her box of Persil just behind the throne."

Daily Express, 22 January 1985

150   George Michael's 1987 single "I Want Your Sex" was banished to post-watershed hours on the radio, amid fears it promoted sexual promiscuity at a time when AIDS was a major concern.

"And my Party's manifesto will remove the BBC's ban on playing George Michael's sex record till after 9 o'clock."

Sunday Express, 24 May 1987

Margaret Thatcher tried hard – ultimately, unsuccessfully – to persuade MPs that letting in television cameras would further damage the reputation of the House of Commons, claiming that radio broadcasting had not enhanced its standing.

"It doesn't surprise me the Leader doesn't want TV cameras in the House."

Daily Express, 11 February 1988

Local Government

More than 10,000 candidates contested local elections in May 1963 and, according to Giles, some were prepared to go to any lengths to be elected.

"Some of us are sure keen to get on that damn council."

Daily Express, 7 May 1963

The Tories had lost seats in council elections earlier in the week, and it appears this former Councillor is not taking the loss well.   153

"Even if he is the Labour candidate who took your seat on the council you've no right to knock his hat off in front of the vicar."

Sunday Express,12 May 1963

One can dream… The upcoming publication of Ian Fleming's 12th James Bond book, *You Only Live Twice*, was in the news. Over 60,000 copies were already pre-ordered.

"This is James Bond, Secret Agent 007, licensed to kill with knife, gun, or bare hand – can I help you?"

Daily Express, 3 March 1964

One imagines that this foolhardy electioneer will soon regret attempting to kidnap redoubtable Grandma.

"You can take a voter to the polling station but you can't make him vote."

Daily Express, 7 April 1964

156 The papers had recently reported the launch of Planning Aid, a free service to help people challenge official planning proposals and those who were adversely affected by road schemes, redevelopment and the like.

"We, the local Council, consider your application to build a kennel for your Fido would constitute a violation of the rural charms of the area."

Daily Express, 6 February 1973

These Councillors, handcuffs at the ready, seem to have a very narrow definition of "nude".

"Wait till he takes his other sock off then we've got him."

Daily Express, 16 August 1973

158 In January, a group of British mercenaries had arrived in Angola to fight in the civil war there. Two days before this cartoon, 44 of them had been flown back to Britain.

"We regret the council is unable to appropriate funds to erect a monument to commemorate your soldier of fortune's weekend in Angola."

Daily Express, 12 February 1976

Having had to apply to the International Monetary Fund for the maximum loan permitted, Chancellor of the Exchequer Denis Healey had announced yet more belt-tightening measures and cuts in public spending.

"I'll please Mr. Healey by cutting out the Rolls, but cut four pages out of my speech I will not!"

Daily Express, 30 November 1976

British Cartoon Archive

All the cartoons in this book were copied from material in Carl Giles's own private archive, a huge collection of artwork, ephemera and correspondence, which is held by the British Cartoon Archive at the University of Kent. Carl Giles had been cartoonist for Lord Beaverbrook's *Daily* and *Sunday Express* for almost 20 years, when on 20 March 1962 the Conservative M.P. Sir Martin Lindsay tabled a motion deploring "the conduct of Lord Beaverbrook in authorizing over the last few years in the newspapers controlled by him more than 70 adverse comments on members of the royal family who have no means of replying."

Lindsay was wrong about the royal family having no means of reply. That day Prince Philip also vented his anger at Beaverbrook's campaign, during a press reception at the British Embassy in Rio de Janeiro. According to the paper's Brazil representative, the Prince declared that, "The *Daily Express* is a bloody awful newspaper. It is full of lies, scandal and imagination. It is a vicious paper."

When the *Daily Express* reported this the next day, Giles decided to treat it as a joke. He knew the royal family enjoyed his cartoons; they often asked for the artwork. This had begun in 1948, when Prince Philip was sent a cartoon on the State Opening of Parliament, and over the next few years Giles received a steady stream of requests from Buckingham Palace for original drawings.

Left: *Lord Beaverbrook is marched to the Tower, 22 March 1962.*

Giles drew the diminutive Lord Beaverbrook being escorted through Traitor's Gate at the Tower of London, with a headsman's axe and block standing ready in the background. The caption repeated Prince Philip's condemnation of the *Daily Express*, but added laconically: "'Ah well,' said Lord B., as they trotted him off to the Tower, 'at least he takes it or he wouldn't know it was a bloody awful newspaper.'"

This was a brilliant response, which did much to defuse the situation. When Giles's cartoon was printed the next day, *Daily Express* staff were surprised to receive a phone call from Queen Elizabeth II's press secretary, with a message for Giles that "Her Majesty requests today's cartoon to commemorate one of her husband's most glorious indiscretions."

Giles sent off the artwork and in May 1962 found himself invited to "a small informal luncheon party" at Buckingham Palace with Queen Elizabeth II and Prince Philip, Duke of Edinburgh. "I was filled with absolute dread," Giles recalled afterwards. "But as soon as she started to talk I was put at my ease...There were about half a dozen corgis running about in a completely uncontrolled state. Suddenly the Queen shouted, 'HEP'. It was like a bark from a sergeant major. The corgis immediately stood to attention. Then filed out of the room."

After the lunch Giles mischievously drew a cartoon of the guests leaving with corgi-savaged trousers. He sent it to the Queen, who returned her thanks through one of her private secretaries, noting that she was "glad that you got away without having lost, at least to the best of her knowledge, so much as a shred of your trousers".

After that Giles became what one *Daily Express* journalist called "a kind of cartooning jester to the royal family". By the time he retired in 1991, the royal family had more than 40 of his original drawings, the largest number being owned by Prince Philip, who shared Giles's anarchic view of the world.

The British Cartoon Archive, based at the University of Kent's Templeman Library in Canterbury, is dedicated to the history of British cartooning over the last 200 years. It holds the artwork for more than 150,000 British political and social-comment cartoons, plus large collections of comic strips, newspaper cuttings, books and magazines. Its catalogue at archive.cartoons.ac.uk includes over 200,000 cartoon images, including the majority of Carl Giles's published works.